Date: 01/31/12

J 599 TOW
Townsend, John,
Incredible mammals /

Incredible
Mammals

John Townsend

Chicago, Illinois

For information, address the publisher:
Raintree, 100 N. LaSalle, Suite 1200, Chicago, IL 60602
Customer Service: 888-363-4266
Visit our website at www.raintreelibrary.com

Printed and bound in China by South China Printing Company.
09 08 07
10 9 8 7 6 5 4 3 2

Library of Congress Cataloging-in-Publication Data
Townsend, John, 1955-
 Incredible mammals / John Townsend.
   p. cm. -- (Incredible creatures)
 Summary: Looks at the behavior and characteristics of different mammals, from the sharp-toothed rodents that dwell throughout most of the world, to the duck-billed platypus that is found only in or near water in Australia.
 Includes bibliographical references and index.
 ISBN 1-4109-0531-4 (lib. bdg.) -- ISBN 1-4109-0855-0 (pbk.)
 ISBN 978-1-4109-0531-4 (lib. bdg.) -- ISBN 978-1-4109-0855-1 (pbk.)
 1. Mammals--Juvenile literature. [1. Mammals.] I. Title.
 QL706.2.T69 2005
 599--dc22
                          2003020292

Acknowledgments
The publishers would like to thank the following for permission to reproduce photographs: p. 4 Anup Shah/Nature Photo Library; pp. 5 (left), 24 Danel Heuclin/NHPA; pp. 5 (top, middle), 12–13, 14 (right), 37 (top) Andy Rouse/NHPA; pp. 5 (bottom), 42 (left) 49 Terry Whittaker/FLPA; pp. 6, 38–39, 42–43 Minden Pictures/FLPA; pp. 6–7 James Warwick/NHPA; p. 7 Helen Rhode/FLPA; p. 8 Martin Harvey/NHPA; pp. 8–9, 23, 44 (left), 44–45, 48 Dave Watts/NHPA; pp. 9, 11 Nick Garbutt/NHPA; p. 10 (left) Brian Bevan/Ardea; pp. 10 (right), 19 Stephen Dalton/NHPA; pp. 12, 20, 46 Photodisc; p. 13, 47 (right) John Shaw/NHPA; p. 14 (left) David E. Meyers/NHPA; p. 15 Martha Holmes/Nature Photo Library; p. 16 T. Kitchin & V. Hurst/NHPA; pp. 16–17 Foto Natura Stock/FLPA; p. 17 Adrian Hepworth/NHPA; pp. 18–19 Sharon Heald/Nature Photo Library; pp. 20–21 Alamy Images; pp. 21, 28 (left), 46–47, 50–51 Martin Harvey/NHPA; pp. 22–23 Panda Photo/FLPA; pp. 24–25 Kevin Schafer/NHPA; pp. 25 (right), 28–29 Daryl Balfour/NHPA; p. 26 Merlin Tuttle, Bat Conservation International/Science Photo Library; pp. 26–27 Tony Wharton/FLPA; p. 27 Barry Mansell/Nature Photo Library; 29 (right) Iain Green/NHPA; pp. 30, 41 Dolphin Institute/Science Photo Library; pp. 30–31 Winfried Wsniewski/FLPA; p. 31 Mark Hamblin/Oxford Scientific Films; p. 32 (left) Jonathan & Angela Scott/NHPA; pp. 32–33 Ant Photo Library/NHPA; p. 34 Mike Johnson; p. 33 (right) Paal Hermansen/NHPA; pp. 34–35, 48–47 Gerard Lacz/FLPA; p. 35 Laurie Campbell/NHPA; pp. 36, 38 Pete Oxford/Nature Photo Library; p. 39 B & C Alexander/NHPA; p. 40 Ron Cohn, kk.org/The Gorilla Foundation; pp. 40–41 F. W. Lane/FLPA; p. 43 (right) P & J Wegner, Foto Natura/FLPA; p. 45 Art Wolfe/Science Photo Library; p. 50 (left) James Carmichael, Jr./NHPA; p. 51 (right) Ann & Steve Toon/NHPA.
Cover photograph of a silverback mountain gorilla reproduced with permission of Steve Bloom.

The publishers would like to thank Mark Rosenthal and Jon Pearce for their assistance in the preparation of this book.

Every effort has been made to contact copyright holders of any material reproduced in this book. Any omissions will be rectified in subsequent printings if notice is given to the publishers.

Disclaimer
All the Internet addresses (URLs) given in this book were valid at the time of going to press. However, due to the dynamic nature of the Internet, some addresses may have changed, or sites may have changed or ceased to exist since publication. While the author and publishers regret any inconvenience this may cause readers, no responsibility for any such changes can be accepted by either the author or the publishers.

The paper used to print this book comes from sustainable resources.

Contents

Some words are shown in **bold.** You can find out what they mean by looking in the glossary. You can also look out for them in the "Wild Words" bank at the bottom of each page.

The World of Mammals

Can you guess what these are?

- The largest mammal can be over 98 ft (30 m) long and weigh more than 140 tons (130 metric tons). That is as big as a jumbo jet. Fifty people could stand on its tongue.

- The tallest mammal can be close to 20 ft (6 m) tall.

- The smallest mammal can be just over 1 in. (3 cm).

- The fastest mammal can move at 60 mi (97 km) per hour.

Answers on page 52.

Mammals are the most advanced form of life on Earth. Many mammals show high intelligence, amazing skills, and the ability to **adapt** to all kinds of places. There are just over 4,000 **species** of mammal. After **amphibians,** mammals make up the smallest group of animals. (Insects have the most species of all.) Yet mammals have taken over the planet. The human mammal has taken charge.

Some mammals spend all their lives in the sea. Others never go near water. Some fly, some live in trees, and some live underground. Most give birth to live young, but a few lay eggs. Most walk on four legs, but some walk on two. Mammals show amazing variety.

▶ Like many mammals, mother leopards lick their young clean.

adapt   gradually change to survive in a particular habitat
mammary glands   parts for making milk in the bodies of female mammals

What are mammals?

All mammals are **vertebrates,** so they have backbones. But so do birds, fish, and **reptiles.** All mammals are **warm-blooded.** That means their bodies stay at the same temperature and do not slow down in the cold. But birds are warm-blooded, too.

So what makes mammals special? There is one main difference: milk. All female mammals produce milk in their bodies to feed their young. This milk comes from **mammary glands,** which is where the word *mammal* comes from.

Scientists put mammals into different groups. Some of these groups are shown in the table below.

Group	Examples
Nibblers and burrowers	rats, mice, and rabbits
Pouched mammals	kangaroos and koalas
Primates	monkeys, apes, and humans
Flying mammals	bats
Insect-eaters	moles and hedgehogs
Grass-eaters	cows, deer, and rhinos
Meat-eaters	lions and wolves
Sea mammals	whales, dolphins, and seals

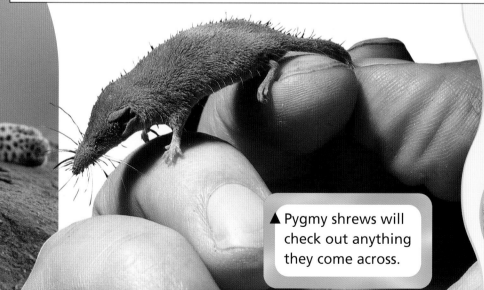

▲ Pygmy shrews will check out anything they come across.

Find out later . . .

Which mammals live in families and look after one another?

Which mammal defends itself with a disgusting trick?

Which mammals might not be around much longer?

species type of animal or plant
vertebrate animal with a backbone

Meet the Family

Nibblers

Rodents make up the largest group of mammals, with more than 1,700 **species**. All rodents have four sharp **incisor** teeth for **gnawing.** These teeth keep growing, but gnawing stops them from getting too long. Rats and mice will gnaw most things, mainly nuts, seeds, and plants, but also anything else they find. Beavers can gnaw through whole trees to make them fall down. Gerbils, guinea pigs, hamsters, squirrels, cavies, chipmunks, and porcupines are also in this group. Rodents live in all **habitats,** from the Arctic to deserts. The largest rodent is the South American capybara, which grows to almost 4.6 ft (1.4 m) long, 23.6 in. (60 cm) tall, and weighs 110 lb (50 kg). That is a little like a guinea pig the size of a large dog.

Long-living rodent

Rodents are easy **prey,** except for the porcupine. They are the longest living of the rodents. They have been known to live for up to 27 years.

▲ Because of their spines, porcupines tend to be left alone.

gland   part of the body that makes hormones and other substances
habitat   natural home of an animal or plant

Rabbits

Rabbits and hares are similar to rodents because they also have large gnawing teeth. Both rodents and rabbits have their eyes on the sides of their heads. This is good for all-around vision. But unlike rodents, rabbits and hares have hair on the soles of their feet and no sweat **glands.**

The official name for this group is *lagomorphs*, which means "leaping shape," and there are about 60 different species. They all have long ears, which give them good hearing and also help to keep them cool. Hares have longer legs and ears than rabbits. They can run over 40 mi (64 km) per hour, often in a zigzag, to get away from a **predator.**

Mammals that are farmers

Pikas such as the one below belong to the rabbit family. There are about fourteen species that live in mountains in Asia, the Middle East, and North America. They gather grass in the summer. They dry and store it so that they have their own hay for the winter.

▲ The capybara is an excellent swimmer and diver.

FAST FACTS

Australia had no rabbits until 24 were taken there from Europe in 1859. Ten years later, there were ten million rabbits in Australia.

incisor   cutting tooth in the front of the mouth
rodent   mammal with gnawing front teeth that keep growing

Pouched mammals

Some mammals have the best way of all to keep their babies safe. They keep them in a pocket on their bodies. **Marsupials** are mammals with pouches for raising their young. They give birth before their babies have developed. The tiny young climb into their mother's pouch. Inside, they spend months feeding on their mother's milk and slowly growing.

Many of the 270 **species** of marsupial come from Australia, such as koalas, possums, wallabies, kangaroos, and wombats. Other marsupials live in New Guinea and South America. The Tasmanian tiger became **extinct** in 1936, although some witnesses think they have spotted one since. It was like a dog with stripes and a pouch. Another marsupial from Tasmania is the Tasmanian devil, which is a small animal like a cat crossed with a bear.

▶ Even young Tasmanian devils can look very tough. They make horrible screeching noises.

evolve   develop and change over time
extinct   died out, never to return

Primates

Primates have larger brains for the size of their bodies than other mammals. They also have hands that can grasp and eyes on the front of their face. There are two groups: lower primates, such as lemurs and bush babies, and higher primates, which are monkeys and apes such as chimpanzees and gorillas. Humans are also in the higher group.

Monkeys have arms and legs of the same length and they use their tails for balancing. A few have tails that can grip like hands. Most monkeys live in tropical forests. Apes are larger and have no tails.

Chimpanzees and gorillas are found only in Africa and are the most highly **evolved** apes. They are some of the most intelligent mammals. Some even learn to use tools.

Big guys

Gorillas are the biggest primate. They are gentle apes that eat fruit and leaves and spend most of the time on the ground. Orangutans such as the one below are the largest mammals to live in trees. They are heavier than humans.

>>>>>>>>>>

Find out more about ape intelligence on page 40.

marsupial mammal with a pouch for raising its young
primate animal with thumbs, eyes on the front of its head, and a large brain

Record-holder 1

The smallest bat in the world is from Thailand and is called Kitti's hog-nosed bat, or the bumblebee bat. It is just 1.2 in. (3 cm) long and weighs less than a coin. This bat is smaller than many insects and competes with the pygmy shrew (shown below) to be the world's smallest mammal.

Bats

Almost a quarter of all mammals can fly. That is because there are about 960 **species** of bats. Some are no bigger than a butterfly, while a Bismarck flying fox can have a **wingspan** of about 6.6 ft (2 m). A bat's wing is different from a bird's because it is covered in thin skin instead of feathers. Bats are the only mammals able to fly steadily. Others, such as flying squirrels, just glide from tree to tree.

There are two main groups of bat:
1. The smaller, insect-eating bats. Some of these also eat frogs and fish. Three species of bat feeds on blood.
2. Fruit bats and flying foxes. These are kind of like small dogs with wings.

▼ The Indian flying fox will fly up to 9 mi (14 km) to find food.

FAST FACTS

Twenty million Mexican free-tail bats from Bracken Cave, Texas, eat 200 tons of insects nightly. They can fly up to 2 mi (3.2 km) high.

Find out more about vampire bats on pages 27 and 43.

insectivore   insect-eater
invertebrate   animal without a backbone

Insect-eaters

Mammals in the **insectivore** group eat mainly insects, but they also feed on other **invertebrates,** such as worms, slugs, and snails. There are about 350 species of these small, very active animals, such as shrews, moles, and hedgehogs. The North American short-tailed shrew has **venom** in its **saliva** to stun insects before it eats them. The pygmy shrew's heart beats more than 800 times a minute. This tiny shrew needs constant energy, so it must keep feeding. If it does not eat for twelve hours, it will die.

Bats and other insectivores eat millions of insects each night. They control some of the worst insect pests.

Record-holder 2

One female tenrec can have up to 32 babies growing inside her at one time. That is more than any other mammal. It is unusual for all of these babies to survive until birth.

▼ The tenrec is a small mammal from Madagascar.

saliva   juices made in the mouth to help chewing and digestion
venom   poison

Grass-eaters

Animals that eat only plants are called **herbivores.** More than 200 **species** of mammals spend most of their time eating grass. Some of these are among the largest land mammals of all. Their toes are very hard and called hooves. Many have long legs and run to escape **predators.**

Some grass-eaters, such as deer, pigs, cattle, giraffes, camels, sheep, goats, and antelopes, have feet with two or four hooves. Others, such as horses, rhinos, and zebras, have an odd number of hooves.

The rhinoceros, hippo, and elephant all eat huge amounts of grass and leaves each day. An elephant can eat 330 to 660 lb (150 to 300 kg) of vegetation a day.

▶ This leopard has just caught a snack. It can kill much larger animals.

carnivore   meat-eater
herbivore   animal that only eats plants

Meat-eaters

Eating grass is hard work. It takes a lot of grass to get even low amounts of energy. Eating meat gives high amounts of **protein**. About 300 species of mammals are hunters and killers. These **carnivores** need to eat meat or fish. Some, such as hyenas, are **scavengers** that often leave the killing to others. Some carnivores may even eat humans.

- Cats are among the most skilled hunters. There are seven species of big cats and 30 species of the smaller wild cats.
- Wolves, wild dogs, and raccoons eat a lot of meat. Wolves learn to hunt together in packs.
- Bears are carnivores, but some eat little meat. Many eat termites. Pandas eat bamboo shoots and only occasionally eat small animals.
- Smaller meat-eating mammals include weasels, skunks, otters, badgers, and mongooses.

Heaviest land carnivores on record

Grizzly bear: 1,700 lb (771 kg)

Polar bear: 1,300 lb (590 kg)

Tiger: 660 lb (300 kg)

American black bear: 600 lb (272 kg)

Lion: 550 lb (250 kg)

▼ A grizzly bear catches salmon as they leap up river.

FAST FACTS

The rhinoceros has the thickest skin of any land mammal. The skin on its back can be 1 in. (2.5 cm) thick. That could stop bullets!

protein   nutrient in food that is used by the body for growth and repair
scavenger   animal that feeds off scraps and prey killed by others

13

Heaviest sea mammals (in tons)

Blue whale: 151
Bowhead whale: 95
Northern right
 whale: 85.6
Fin whale: 70
Sperm whale: 48.2

Sea mammals

Some of the largest and most intelligent mammals live in the sea. They breathe air and feed their young on milk like all other mammals. There are about 75 **species** of whales, dolphins, and porpoises. Many live in groups called schools, and they keep in touch through "songs" that can be heard for several miles under the sea. Beluga whales are called sea canaries because their songs sound like canaries singing.

The largest **predator** on the planet is the sperm whale. It can dive more than half a mile deep to catch giant squid. This can often result in a violent fight to the death. The whales are able to stay below water for up to an hour before they must rise to the surface to breathe air.

▲ Even the tail of a blue whale is huge. It can be 23 to 33 ft (7–10 m) across.

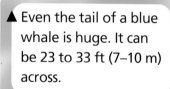

FAST FACTS

An adult blue whale can eat more than 40 million krill in one day. That is over 3 tons.

▲ Bottle-nosed dolphins can jump up to 20 ft (6 m) out of the water.

blubber layers of fat that protect whales and seals and keep them warm
krill tiny shrimplike animals that swim in large numbers in the sea

Whales and dolphins

Dolphins and porpoises can keep swimming for several hours at 25 mi (40 km) per hour. In this way, they cover long distances in their search for fish. They often work together to "round up" large numbers of fish before they swoop in for the kill.

Some whales feed by taking in huge gulps of water and fish at the same time. Killer whales hunt large **prey** such as seals and other whales. They rarely attack humans and can actually be very gentle with people. Other whales are filter feeders and swim with their mouths open to strain small, shrimplike **krill** from the sea.

▼ The bowhead whale has the thickest fat of any animal.

---

predator   animal that hunts and eats other animals
prey   animal that is killed and eaten by other animals

Crowded beach

Walruses gather together in huge numbers to breed. Sometimes 3,000 of them crowd together on the rocks, with hardly any room to move. A male walrus can be more than 11.5 ft (3.5 m) long. He can guard about 50 females against other males, using his tusks to protect them.

Flipper feet

Another group of sea mammals includes seals, sea lions, and walruses. Most eat fish and some, such as leopard seals, eat penguins. These are all fast swimmers, but many struggle to move easily on land. They are all well **adapted** to life in water, yet most must come to shore to **breed.** Only manatees and dugongs can breed in the water. These slow mammals are called sea cows, and they graze on plants in the water.

Elephant seals can weigh a huge 7,700 lb (3,500 kg), while walruses can reach 2,650 lb (1,200 kg). A male walrus grows tusks that can measure 3.3 ft (1 m) long. Not only are these useful for raking shellfish from the seabed, but they are also dangerous weapons for use against other walruses or a hungry polar bear.

algae   types of simple plant without stems that grow in water or wet places

Odds and ends

There are a few strange mammals that stand out as being different. A few slower-moving mammals with small teeth, or no teeth at all, are part of one small group. These are the sloths, anteaters, and armadillos. Anteaters are the only mammals that have no teeth. They use their long, sticky tongue to flick into ant nests and lick out hundreds of ants at a time. The giant anteater eats over ten million ants or termites a year. Armadillos and pangolins have bony armor to protect them.

Most mammals give birth to live young. However, there are three **species** of mammal that lay eggs. One is the duck-billed platypus, and the other two are echidnas, which are beaked anteaters. These are certainly the "odd ones out" in the whole mammal family.

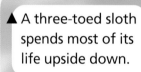

▲ A three-toed sloth spends most of its life upside down.

>>>> Find out more about the strange platypus on page 44.

◄ A dugong feeding on the seabed. Its closest living relative is the elephant.

No hurry

There are five species of sloth that live in the trees of South America. These hairy mammals hang upside down from hooklike claws. They are very slow. The normal speed of a three-toed sloth is about 6.6 ft (2 m) per minute. They are so slow that **algae** has time to grow in their hair, so they can look greenish in color.

breed   produce offspring

Amazing Bodies

Running records

- In 2002 Tim Montgomery sprinted 109 yd (100 m) at 22.9 mi (36.8 km) per hour to take the world record.

- A cheetah, such as the one below, can go from 0 to 60 mi (96 km) per hour in under three seconds. That is faster than a Ferrari! Cheetahs can only run fast in short bursts up to 550 yd (500 m).

Mammals are among the most successful animals because they have **evolved** all kinds of body shapes to **adapt** to different **habitats.**

Designs for living

Whether they live in oceans, jungles, mountains, deserts, or on ice caps, mammals can survive very well in their **environment.** Even mammals that live far inland can swim well. Hamsters fill their cheek pouches with air before taking the plunge.

Some **species,** such as otters, beavers, and hippos, are just as much at home in the water as on land. Most land mammals swim by dog-paddling—they just make walking movements while floating in the water.

FAST FACTS

Fastest mammals (top speed)
1st Cheetah
65 mi (104 km)
per hour
2nd Pronghorn antelope
55 mi (88 km)
per hour
3rd Springbok
50 mi (80 km)
per hour
4th Gazelles
(various kinds)
47 mi (76 km)
per hour

environment   natural surroundings
limb   arm or leg

Flesh and bones

All mammals depend on a strong backbone. This spine, as with other **vertebrates,** is made of many small bones with one or more hole through the center. These holes are lined up to make a tube. The tube protects the spinal cord, which is a "rope" of **nerves.** The spinal cord carries signals to and from the brain all around the body.

Mammals' bodies remain at a steady temperature. They burn food to keep warm and stay cool by sweating or panting. Land mammals are **unique** in having hair to help them stay at the right temperature. Even humans are covered in tiny hairs. Many mammals grow a thick coat of hair during winter, which they lose for a much thinner one during summer.

The glider

A flying squirrel (shown below) has a body designed for gliding through the trees. It does not actually fly, but simply stretches out its **limbs.** The skin that flaps between its limbs traps the air and acts like a hang glider as the squirrel sails from tree to tree.

◀ Hippos spend most of the day in water, then graze on land at night.

nerves   fibers that carry messages between the brain and other parts of the body
unique   only one of its kind; nothing else like it

Big-hearted

- A blue whale's heart is the size of a small car. It has to pump 10.7 tons (9.7 metric tons) of blood around its huge body.

- A giraffe's heart weighs more than 24 lb (11 kg) and is 23.6 in. (60 cm) long. The heart's **muscular** walls are up to 2.8 in. (7 cm) thick, since it has to pump blood to quite a height.

Breathing

All mammals breathe air. Their lungs take in **oxygen,** which is taken around the body by the blood. Whales and dolphins need to swim up to the surface of the sea to breathe in and out. As they breathe out **carbon dioxide,** they push up a spout of water that shoots many feet into the air. Every few minutes, they blow out and take in a breath of fresh air.

Other sea mammals also have to surface to take breaths. Seals can dive deep underwater and hold their breath for up to twenty minutes, but they must return to the surface to breathe. A seal's heart rate slows down when it is underwater, from about 100 beats a minute to just 10. This helps it to stay underwater without needing too much oxygen.

carbon dioxide   gas that animals breathe out
hibernate   "close down" the body and rest when it is too cold or dry

Heart rates

All mammals' hearts have four **chambers** for taking in and pumping out blood. When resting, the adult human heart pumps out about 1 gal (4 l) of blood per minute. A horse's heart pumps about 5.3 gal (20 l), but this goes up to 14 gal (53 l) per minute when the horse gallops.

Mammals' hearts slow down when they **hibernate.** A hedgehog has a normal heart rate of between 200 and 280 beats per minute. This goes down to 147 while it is asleep. It then drops to about 5 beats per minute when the hedgehog is hibernating. The heart rate of a medium-sized bat can go from 700 beats per minute when it is resting to 1,000 when it is flying to just 25 beats per minute when it hibernates.

Average heart rate of mammals at rest (beats per minute)

Elephant:	35
Lion:	40
Human:	70
Rabbit:	200
Mouse:	600
Shrew:	800

To find your heart rate, you just need a stopwatch or watch with a second hand. Sit still for a while and find your pulse in your neck or wrist. Count the number of beats in 60 seconds.

◀ The heart of a galloping horse can beat up to 250 times per minute.

muscular   having strong muscles
oxygen   one of the gases in air and water that all living things need

Sound waves

- Dolphins and bats use high-pitched sounds that we cannot hear. They pick up the echoes of these sounds, which bounce off objects around them. This helps them find their way. It is called **echolocation.**

- Giraffes and elephants look as though they are just quietly **grazing** on the African plains. In fact, they may be "talking" over long distances. They make and hear sounds that we cannot hear. Scientists are studying the **infrasonic** sounds some mammals make.

Two European wolves focus on likely prey.

Senses

Like every animal on the planet, mammals need senses to figure out what is going on around them. They must know about danger, food, or a partner. Most mammals have five senses: sight, hearing, smell, taste, and touch. In some mammals, one of these senses is developed into a super-sense, far better than our own.

echolocation   bouncing high-pitched sounds off objects to figure out where to go
infrasonic   very low-pitched sounds that humans cannot hear

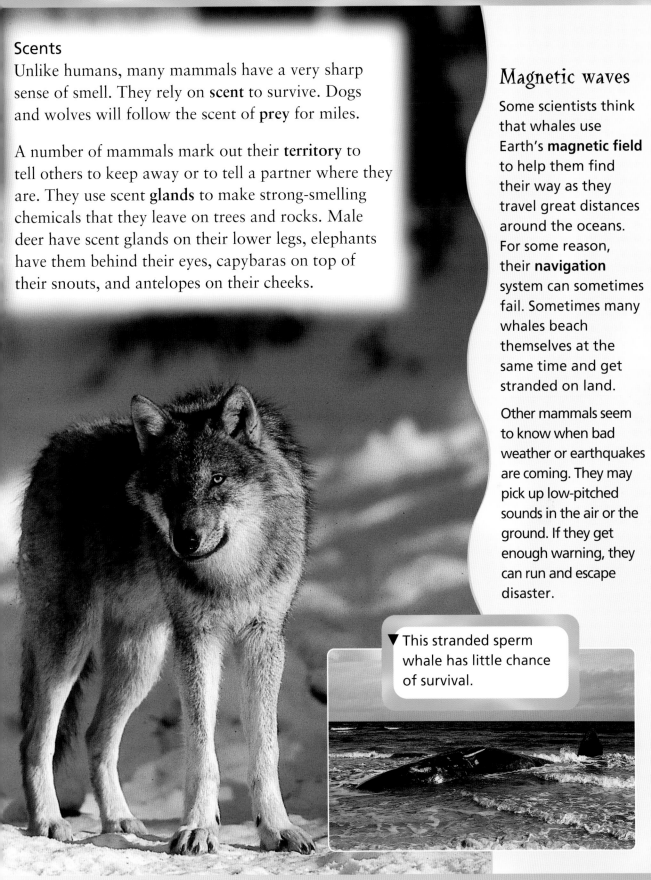

Scents

Unlike humans, many mammals have a very sharp sense of smell. They rely on **scent** to survive. Dogs and wolves will follow the scent of **prey** for miles.

A number of mammals mark out their **territory** to tell others to keep away or to tell a partner where they are. They use scent **glands** to make strong-smelling chemicals that they leave on trees and rocks. Male deer have scent glands on their lower legs, elephants have them behind their eyes, capybaras on top of their snouts, and antelopes on their cheeks.

Magnetic waves

Some scientists think that whales use Earth's **magnetic field** to help them find their way as they travel great distances around the oceans. For some reason, their **navigation** system can sometimes fail. Sometimes many whales beach themselves at the same time and get stranded on land.

Other mammals seem to know when bad weather or earthquakes are coming. They may pick up low-pitched sounds in the air or the ground. If they get enough warning, they can run and escape disaster.

▼ This stranded sperm whale has little chance of survival.

magnetic field   pulling force from Earth's North and South poles
scent   trail left by an animal that others can smell and follow

Feeding

All animals need to get **nutrients** into their bodies to renew and repair **cells.** Food also gives mammals energy to keep them active—so they must eat often. Unlike many **reptiles** and insects, mammals cannot last for long periods without eating. Even so, some mammals, such as bears and seals, are able to get energy from their own fat supplies when they cannot find food.

Herbivores

Herbivores must eat grass and leaves each day to keep up their energy levels. This can be a problem at times of the year when there are fewer plants to eat. **Grazing** mammals have to get the maximum **nourishment** from grass. To do this, they chew their food over and over again, and their stomach is divided into several **chambers.**

Did you know . . . ?

Camels can survive for days without food and water. When a camel finally gets to drink, it can gulp down 13.2 gallons (50 liters) in a few minutes. Most of its body fat is in its hump, so the rest of its body can keep cool. Bactrian camels have two humps. These herbivores make good use of whatever plants they can find to eat.

▼ Elephants eat up to 21 hours a day.

digestive system   organs in the body that break down food to absorb nutrients
graze   eat grass and plants

Digesting plants

For some herbivores, a large stomach called a **rumen** stores half-eaten grass. Cows, deer, and camels can then bring the grass back up into their mouths and chew it. They eat their dinner all over again!

Not all herbivores eat like this. Horses and kangaroos have a very long **digestive system.** This is to make sure that as much nourishment as possible is absorbed from the grass, leaves, or shoots. Other herbivores feed on seeds or fruits. These provide a far richer diet than leaves. They contain many more sugars, fats, and **proteins. Rodents** eat mainly seeds and nuts. A lot of mammals, such as **primates** and tropical bats, live on fruit.

Big eater

Elephants walk several miles looking for leaves, bark, grass, and fruit as well as 21 gallons (80 liters) of water per day. A herd of elephants can destroy a whole field of crops very quickly, which is why it is important to manage the number of elephants carefully.

▲ Howler monkeys in Brazil eat a lot of fruit.

nourishment important nutrients provided by food
nutrient important substance found in food and needed by the body

Insects and other **invertebrates** are a rich source of food for many mammals because they are packed with **protein.** Some **insectivores,** such as shrews, many bats, anteaters, and aardvarks, eat nothing but insects. Although spiders and snails are not insects, they are also on the menu for most insectivores. For many mammals, grubs, bugs, worms, snails, and spiders make up a large part of their diet. Moles, foxes, badgers, mongooses, and skunks, as well as many **primates** and **rodents,** will eat lots of insects each day. And as moles burrow through dirt, they hunt down all kinds of creatures that live in the soil. Moles will eat earthworms, beetles, flies, millipedes, moths, and ants.

Can you believe it?

Bats are very important in controlling insects. They eat many harmful insects, such as mosquitoes. In just one evening, a bat **colony** can eat half a million flies. Over a year, that is a huge amount of insects.

▲ Hundreds of bats come out to feed at sunset.

► This mole has caught an earthworm.

carrion   dead, rotting flesh
colony   large group of animals living together

Omnivores

Strictly speaking, many mammals are **omnivores**. This means that they eat a mixture of plants, insects, and meat. The meat may be small mammals, **reptiles,** fish, or **carrion.** Rats, for example, will eat anything. Their **digestive systems** cope with all kinds of material.

Many primates, including humans, are omnivores. Chimpanzees will eat fruit, leaves, monkeys, wild pigs, and termites. Smaller primates feed on whatever they can find, from fruits, seeds, and leaves to insects, birds, and their eggs. A few primates, such as gorillas, are **herbivores.** Of all the primates, only humans and chimpanzees hunt in groups to find large-sized **prey.**

Blood-thirsty bats

Not all bats eat just insects. Vampire bats such as the one below need about two tablespoonfuls of blood each night. It takes about twenty minutes for this small South American mammal to drink the blood from cattle, horses, or birds. Its **saliva** keeps the blood flowing while it licks its meal. This does not cause any harm to the animal bitten—unless the bat has **rabies.**

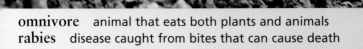

omnivore   animal that eats both plants and animals
rabies   disease caught from bites that can cause death

Teamwork

Hunting and chasing prey uses up a lot of energy. More often than not, the prey escapes and the carnivore is left hungry and **exhausted**. That is why many animals, such as lions, hyenas, and wolves, prefer teamwork. Working together saves energy and is a good way of feeding the whole group.

Carnivores

Carnivores have developed teeth like scissor blades to cut up meat. They use four special pointed **incisor** teeth for killing large **prey**. Big cats bite the throat of their victim. This clamps the prey's windpipe so that it **suffocates,** or it can break the prey's spinal cord. Then the feeding starts as the carnivore rips off small chunks of meat. These chunks tend to be swallowed whole, rather than chewed very much. Many cats have a rough tongue that can scrape meat off the bones.

All carnivores have strong jaws, powerful jaw muscles, and heavy skulls to put their teeth into action. The jaguar of South America has some of the strongest jaws. This big cat can even bite through a turtle's tough shell.

▶ Lionesses often hunt together to pull down large prey such as this buffalo.

▼ Packs of hyenas hunt together.

exhausted   worn out, with all energy gone
marrow   soft, fatty jelly inside bones

Big killers

Hyenas from Africa and southern Asia hunt in packs, but they also clean up after other carnivores. These strong, doglike animals have powerful jaws and teeth for ripping skin, flesh, and chewy bits. They also have sharp, pointed teeth for crushing bones to get to the **marrow** inside.

But it is the cat family that has many of the most skilled killers. Their bursts of speed, strength, and biting power make them great **predators.** Razor claws that flick out to attack also help them catch and kill animals far bigger than themselves. Big cats are found all around the world, except for Australia, Antarctica, and some islands. The tiger is the largest species and is the "**ultimate** killing machine."

Man-eaters

Over the last 400 years, it is thought that tigers have killed over one million people. Humans make easy prey. In India, people who went into the forests to cut timber were often attacked from behind.

▼ Tigers go for the throat of their prey.

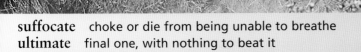

suffocate   choke or die from being unable to breathe
ultimate   final one, with nothing to beat it

Breeding

Mating

When mammals mate, the male needs to place **sperm** inside the female. If she releases egg **cells** from her **ovaries,** these will meet the sperm in her **oviduct**. When egg and sperm meet here, **fertilization** takes place. New life begins and a baby mammal starts to grow.

The best time to raise a family depends on the **species** and where it lives. Most baby mammals are helpless when they are born, so they need to be taken care of for some time.

Meeting and mating

Spring is often the best time to be born, when the weather and food supply mean that cubs and calves have a better chance of survival. So adults are often **programmed** to find a partner at a particular time: the mating season. This is when females show they are ready to **mate** and males fight among themselves to show which is the fittest.

Scent plays a key part in bringing males and females together. The female's scent tells males she is looking for a partner.

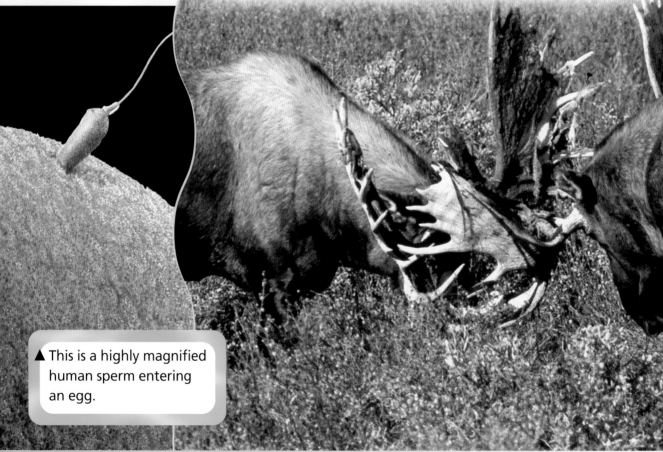

▲ This is a highly magnified human sperm entering an egg.

ovary   part of the female's body where the eggs are made
oviduct   tube inside a female down which her eggs pass

Finding a mate

Male orangutans call to females across the jungles of Sumatra and Borneo. They shake branches with a loud roar to keep other males away. A female orangutan is very choosy and looks for the largest male.

The moose is one of North America's largest land mammals. The bulls (males) go through a lot of trouble to find a mate. They travel many miles, mark **territory,** and fight like crazy. This is called the fall **rut,** when males lock antlers and get aggressive. They may break their antlers and get hurt. When a bull finally wins a female, they mate very quickly. Then it is all over until the next year.

▼ Bull moose lock antlers in the mating season.

Timing

Not all animals have a set **breeding** season. If some mammals mate in the summer, their fertilized egg does not develop right away. This is to avoid giving birth to the baby in winter, when it might die. If stoats such as the one below mate in summer, the fertilized egg goes "on hold" until the next spring, when it will then grow and be born.

programmed   has behavior that is "built in" or automatic
sperm   male sex cell

Gestation

Gestation is the time from **fertilization** to birth. Below are some gestation times.

African elephant: 660 days (nearly 2 years)

Beaked whale: 520 days

Human: 275 days

Chimpanzee: 237 days

Lion: 108 days

Mouse: 21 days

Birth

A fertilized egg grows inside the female's **uterus.** A tiny ball of **cells** begins to form into a baby mammal. This is the **embryo.** It is connected to the uterus by a cord called the **umbilical cord.** This cord links the embryo to the **placenta,** which is a special organ that feeds the baby. The placenta takes all the food and **oxygen** that the embryo needs from the mother's blood. At the same time, it passes back the embryo's wastes, such as **carbon dioxide.** The wastes are taken away in the mother's blood. The embryo's lungs only begin to work when it is born into the fresh air.

▼ Young African elephants need their mother for eight to ten years.

embryo   tiny group of growing cells formed from a fertilized egg
placenta   organ inside a pregnant female mammal that feeds the growing baby

Mother bonding

When baby mammals are born, the first thing their mother will do is clean them. She will lick them dry and cut the umbilical cord by biting through it near the baby's body. It will not bleed because the umbilical cord stops working at birth. The mothers of many wild mammals quickly eat the placenta and umbilical cord. This is important because the blood in the placenta could attract **predators** to the new, helpless offspring. The placenta is also full of **nutrients** that the mother does not want to waste.

When she licks her young for the first time, the mother also gets to know their smell. This is important for mammals that live in herds such as deer, sheep, or horses. In this way, they bond right away.

Amazing!

Female lemmings can become pregnant at fourteen days old. The gestation period is from 16 to 23 days. One pair of lemmings such as the one below once produced eight litters in 167 days.

◄ A mother cleans her newly born foal (baby horse). The foal will soon be up on its feet.

umbilical cord   cord that joins the embryo to the placenta inside the mother
uterus   womb; where a baby grows inside its mother

33

Milk and mothers

Milk is the mammal's magic liquid. Newborn babies have an instant supply of liquid food on tap. No other animals have this special way of feeding their young. Milk is a rich mixture of water, **proteins,** fats, and vitamins.

Some mammals' milk is high in protein to help the young grow fast. This is important for **grazing** animals that have to be on their feet quickly. Other mammals' milk is extra high in fat so the baby gains weight rapidly. Seal milk is high in fat so that the babies can quickly build up a layer of **blubber.** This is important because they often live in cold climates and have to swim in icy seas. When they have enough fat, they shed their baby fur.

Whale milk

In seven months of giving milk to her calf (baby), a female blue whale can lose up to a quarter of her body weight. A blue whale calf drinks over 59 gal (225 l) of its mother's milk in a day. In its first few weeks, it gains almost 9 lb (4 kg) an hour.

▼ A blue whale calf will stay close to its mother until it is weaned.

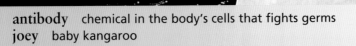

antibody   chemical in the body's cells that fights germs
joey   baby kangaroo

Making milk

Producing milk can put a strain on the mother. She has to eat well to make enough milk. If food or water is short, she will stop producing milk. This means her young will die, but it gives her a chance to survive.

Kangaroos often have two babies, called **joeys,** of different ages needing milk at the same time. One will be tiny and one will be nearly **weaned.** The mother produces two types of milk from the two teats used by the two joeys. The youngest will be attached to one teat for its first few weeks. This milk has very little fat in it. Its older brother or sister will get another milk mixture. This has almost 20 percent fat, so the joey gains weight before it hops from the pouch.

▼ A harp seal pup is helpless as it lies in the snow.

Milk fat

A reindeer's milk has to be extra high in fat. The calf (baby) must put on weight fast to protect it from the cold weather. A horse foal (baby), on the other hand, has longer to grow in warmer weather. Milk is also full of **antibodies** to help the young fight disease.

▲ Reindeer milk is very high in fat.

weaned   coming off mother's milk

Weird and Wonderful

It is a tough world out there. There are many **predators** that eat mammals.

Thick-skinned

Not much can get through the armor of a three-banded armadillo. It also sometimes leaves a small opening in the armor plates that snaps shut on a predator's paw or snout. That soon sends the hunter packing.

Defense

There are all kinds of ways to put up a fight and not get eaten.

Camouflage

One way to succeed in the jungle is to disappear. **Camouflage** is the best way to keep out of sight. Camouflage is important for both the hunted and the hunter. A leopard's spotted fur is excellent for blending into the undergrowth. It just cannot be seen. On the other hand, a herd of stripy zebra can look confusing to a predator, which finds it hard to pick out one animal to attack. Many mammals that live on ice and snow have white fur. This makes them very hard to see, so they stay safe.

► It is possible to smell a skunk from a long way away.

▲ Three-banded armadillos just roll into a ball when a predator comes near.

camouflage   color or pattern that matches the background

Kicking up a stink

If a hunter threatens an opossum, it pretends to be dead. It even lets off a smell to make an attacker think it is dead meat. That is enough to make anyone leave it alone.

The animal that makes the worst smell of all has to be the skunk. There are three types of skunk: striped, hog-nosed, and spotted. They live in North, Central, and South America. Most skunks warn predators by stamping their feet and raising their tail. If that fails, they spray a liquid at the predator's face, which can cause blindness for a while. And it stinks.

A skunk has two **glands** under its tail. These spray out foul-smelling fluid up to about 10 feet (3 meters). Its smell is so strong that an attacker can hardly breathe. So beware if you see one!

▼ This Indian mongoose is attacking a cobra.

Building defenses

A mongoose eats lizards and snakes, even deadly ones. The diet of poison slowly builds up the mongoose's defense against snake **venom.** An older mongoose can even survive a cobra bite that would kill a human. A young mongoose must be more careful until its natural defenses build up.

High and hot

- The camel is at home in hot deserts. Its large toes stop it from sinking into hot sand. If there is a sandstorm, it just lies down and closes up its nostrils and extra eyelids.

- The yak of Tibet and China can climb up to over 19,650 ft (6,000 m) in the freezing mountains. This makes it the mammal that lives at the highest **altitude.**

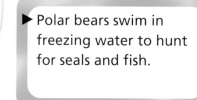
▼ The yak's long, shaggy coat keeps it warm.

Extremes

Our planet can be an unfriendly place. Some parts are bitterly cold and thick with ice or freezing water. Other places are scorching hot and dry where the burning sun beats down. But mammals survive at these extremes. Some live high up in steep mountains, and some are at home in dark, underground caves.

In the Arctic winters, polar bears can cope with some of the coldest temperatures. Females dig themselves into dens under the snow, where they give birth and stay throughout the winter. They keep just enough blood in their feet to stop their toes from freezing. Their thick fur is made of hollow hairs that trap heat.

▶ Polar bears swim in freezing water to hunt for seals and fish.

altitude   height above sea level

Cold and hot

Many mammals grow thicker fur in the winter. A reindeer's winter coat can be 6 in. (15 cm) thick. This will slow down heat loss from the skin even when the air temperature drops to −22 °F (−30 °C). Thick hair does not work so well when it is wet. To solve this problem, otters and beavers have very thick **water-repellent** fur, which keeps warm air trapped next to their skin.

The oryx is a type of antelope that is **adapted** to life in hot deserts. It can cope with high body temperatures that would quickly kill other mammals. It is able to cool down at night so the heat of the day does not bother it. Even if its body temperature rises to 113 °F (45 °C), it does not sweat.

Icy survivors

Whales are able to survive in very cold seas. Their thick layers of **blubber** keep them warm in freezing water full of icebergs.

FAST FACTS

Polar bears are not really white. Their skin is black and their clear hair reflects light, which makes them appear white.

water-repellent   able to keep water out

Cyber ape

A gorilla named Koko started sign language training more than twenty years ago. After two months, she could string words together, such as "more food" and "more drink." In 1998 Koko became the first nonhuman mammal to communicate via the Internet. In the photo below, she is using a computer to make the sign for "apple."

Problem solvers

Mammal brains can do some quick thinking. Unlike some animals, many mammals can figure things out and solve simple problems. Some care for others and even show sadness or grief.

Mammals have bigger brains in relation to their bodies than other animals. This means that they can learn about their **environment.** Baby **reptiles,** fish, and **amphibians** tend to be left to fend for themselves. This means they have to find food on their own right away and have little time to learn through play or to be taught by parents. Because baby mammals are fed and looked after, they have more time to develop. They have longer to explore and find out about their surroundings, pick up behavior from their mother, and develop more complex brains.

▼ Chimpanzees figure out how to use simple tools to get what they want.

amphibian   animal with a backbone that lives in water and on land, such as a frog

Chimp intelligence

Apes can be quick to learn new skills. A lot of work has been done to teach chimpanzees to "speak" using grunts and sign language. Some have learned to push different buttons in response to certain words. They can show understanding of many different signs.

A female chimpanzee named Washoe learned to use more than 100 signs from American Sign Language. In the early 1970s, she was by a lake and saw a swan for the first time. She did not know a sign for swan, so she thought about it. The people who trained her were amazed when she put together two signs to describe the swan. Washoe used her hands to sign "water bird." That shows complex thinking.

Smart dolphins

Dolphins learn all kinds of tricks. They can figure out different shapes and colors in puzzles. Scientists believe they can even recognize themselves in mirrors. In the wild, dolphins often pick up lumps of sponge and put them on their noses to protect them from sea snakes as they dig for food. That shows brain power.

▲ These dolphins are learning sign language.

reptile   cold-blooded animal with scales, such as a snake or lizard

Caring for each other

Marmosets such as the ones below search for food as a family and they share it—often right out of one other's mouths! Older brothers and sisters help with the babysitting by feeding, carrying, teaching, and protecting the babies of the family.

Close friends

Living in families and groups makes sense. It means more eyes are on the lookout for danger or food. There is safety in numbers. Not only that—some mammals seem to need the friendship of others. They soon become bored on their own.

Many mammals that live in groups show that they can recognize each other. They also remember a lot of information about individuals. After all, they need to know who is boss, who is related to whom, and who has done what to whom in the past. Baby mammals growing up with other young can play and learn together. Often, parents are able to keep an eye on other young in the group and share the babysitting duties.

▶ Two adult bottle-nosed dolphins care for a calf (baby).

midwife   nurse who helps a mother when she gives birth

Showing concern for others

When a female dolphin begins to give birth, she may make a strange whistling sound. This is a signal that means "help." A **midwife** dolphin will often arrive. She helps the mother push the newborn dolphin to the surface for its first breath of air. The midwife also helps the mother protect the young from sharks for several weeks after its birth.

Vampire bats can also support each other by sharing food. These animals live life on the edge. If a bat fails to find blood, it may not live to see the next night's hunting. A bat that has fed well will have more than enough blood to survive. So sometimes a full bat will **regurgitate** some of its meal to feed another bat that is starving.

Monkey business

Monkeys, baboons, and other mammals groom each other. This does not just help them keep clean. Grooming is a sign of friendship that may say, "I care about you."

FAST FACTS

Humans have special names for groups of animals—for example, a pride of lions and a pack of wolves. Have you heard of:
- a lodge of beavers;
- a tower of giraffes;
- a leap of leopards;
- a labor of moles;
- a huddle of walruses;
- a zeal of zebras?

▼ Baboons groom each other to bond.

regurgitate   throw up digested food

Laying eggs

- Only two families of mammal are **monotremes:** mammals that lay eggs. They are echidnas and platypuses.

- The female duck-billed platypus lays her eggs at the end of a tunnel. They hatch after about ten days. The offspring feed on their mother's milk for three to four months.

Monotremes

The duck-billed platypus is a very strange mammal. When Europeans first saw a stuffed one, they thought someone had sewn a duck's beak onto a mammal's body for a joke. The duck-billed platypus has a brown, fur-covered body, short webbed feet, and a large beak, like a duck's **bill.**

The word *platypus* is Greek for "flat feet." Although it does not move easily on land, the platypus is a great swimmer. It looks for food at the bottom of lakes and rivers by using its bill to detect the presence of small shrimp and crabs. The males have poisonous spikes on their rear ankles. They use them for defense or in fighting rival males for a partner.

▶ A large **joey** still crams itself into its mother's pouch when danger threatens.

▼ The duck-billed platypus lives in and around water in Australia.

bill   jaws and beak of a bird

Marsupials

Mammals with pockets are also unusual. Having your own baby-carrier can be very handy.

The word *marsupial* comes from the Latin word *marsupium*, which means "little bag." The **embryos** of marsupials only spend 12 to 28 days in their mother's **uterus.** When they are born, marsupial babies are very small and totally helpless. The gray kangaroo is only 0.03 oz (0.8 g) at birth and looks like a worm. It can grow to be over 66 lb (30 kg) as an adult.

The baby marsupial has to leave its mother's uterus, crawl up her belly, and get into her pouch. It gets no help, so it is a real struggle. Once inside the pouch, the baby finds a teat to supply it with milk. Even a one-year-old kangaroo will hop back in the pouch if it gets scared.

Joey

When a joey leaves it mother's pouch, it weighs 11 lb (5 kg). The young kangaroo keeps drinking its mother's milk until it is about eighteen months old. At this age it is almost too big to get in the pouch anymore.

◀ The baby gray kangaroo spends 300 days in its mother's pouch.

Bison journeys across America

Like many mammals, bison are ruled by the seasons. Herds move to new pastures every winter to find better **grazing**.

▼ Bison are the largest land mammals in North America.

On the move

Animals that live in large groups may benefit from safety in numbers, but there are more mouths to feed. Once they have eaten all their supplies, they have to go on the move to find more food. Many mammals have a pattern of **migration** that they repeat every year.

Gray whales migrate in small groups of up to ten. They swim north to the Arctic for summer feeding and south to warm water to rest and give birth in winter. It is thought that they may make the longest migrations of any mammal—up to 10,000 miles (16,000 kilometers) each year.

Californian gray whales migrate along the western coast of North America. In the summer they feed in the Arctic. As winter approaches, they head toward the lagoons of Mexico, where they give birth.

▶ A wildebeest herd crosses the Mara River in Kenya, Africa.

migration   traveling long distances in search of food or to breed

Wildebeest

Every year more than a million wildebeest and 200,000 zebras move across the Serengeti Plain of East Africa. They migrate over 1,800 miles (2,900 kilometers) each year in search of grass. They are followed by groups of big cats looking for **prey**.

When the dry season comes, vast herds of wildebeest set off in search of fresh grass. They are most active in the mornings and rest during the heat of the day and at night. There is no end to a wildebeest's journey. Its life is a constant search for food and water. Herds sometimes have to cross dangerous rivers. About 400,000 wildebeest calves (babies) are born over a six-week period, early each year. Calves can stand and run within five minutes of being born. The weaker calves do not survive the journey.

Not on the move

Here is a list of the sleepiest mammals and the average number of hours they sleep each day. How much sleep do you get?

Koala (shown below):	22
Sloth:	20
Armadillo:	19
Opossum:	19
Lemur:	16
Hamster:	14
Squirrel:	14
Cat:	13
Pig:	13

FAST FACTS

Some sloths, armadillos, and opossums spend up to 80 percent of their lives dozing. It is claimed that the Dall's porpoise never sleeps at all.

Mammals in Danger

A close shave

The New Zealand southern right whale was once thought to be extinct. It has been rediscovered near the Auckland Islands, 200 mi (322 km) south of New Zealand. There could now be about 150 of these whales able to **breed.** Maybe this mammal (shown below) will be saved before it is too late.

About 30 **species** of mammal have become **extinct** in the last 200 years. There used to be a species of lion known as the Barbary lion that lived in North Africa. They were much bigger than today's African lions. These were the lions that ancient Roman **gladiators** used to fight in their sports arenas. But the forests where these lions lived were chopped down to make way for farming. Animals disappeared, including the lions' **prey.** The Barbary lions were soon gone, too. The last Barbary lion was seen in the 1920s.

Almost 150 mammal species today are rare or in danger of being lost forever. The destruction of **habitats,** especially rain forests, and hunting have pushed many mammals to the brink of extinction.

▶ The giant panda is the symbol for the **WWF,** which works to save endangered species.

endangered   at risk of disappearing forever
gladiator   person in ancient Rome who would fight for others' entertainment

On the brink

Perhaps the best-known **endangered** mammal is the giant panda. This magnificent animal lives in the forests of China, where it mainly eats bamboo shoots. However, humans have cleared large areas of bamboo, so pandas can no longer find food. Efforts are now being made to save the panda.

Tigers have been hunted for years and are now at great risk. There are only 400 Siberian tigers left in the wild. India has the greatest number of tigers, but even these Bengal tigers are down to 4,500.

More than 4,000 koalas are killed every year in Australia. Habitat destruction, dogs, cars, bush fires, and hunting have reduced the koala population from more than three million a century ago to less than 100,000 today.

Rare

- The northern hairy-nosed wombat is the largest burrowing **herbivore.** Today it is one of the world's rarest mammals. It is now only found in eastern Queensland, Australia.

- The most endangered large mammal is the Sumatran rhinoceros. There are fewer than 300 left. The other four species of rhino (white, black, Indian, and Javan) are in danger because they are **poached** for their horns.

◄ This male Sumatran rhino is in danger of disappearing forever.

poach illegally kill and steal wild animals
WWF World Wildlife Federation

49

Human-made mammals

While the zoos in the world are fighting to conserve endangered animals, some scientists have crossbred mammals in the hope of learning more about their **genes**.

Humans

The human mammal is the main threat to other mammals on the planet. Yet humans' skills may help to solve some of the problems. Scientists are working hard to protect **endangered species** and to help increase small populations of mammals. People can protect animal **habitats** by setting up reserves and special **conservation** areas. We can also protect endangered species by **breeding** animals in zoos. The Arabian oryx, which was once **extinct** in the wild, has been successfully bred in zoos, and several hundred have been released into protected habitats. Humans can also set up laws to prevent **poaching** and **pollution**.

- Did you know there are mammals such as tigons (shown above)? They are lions crossed with tigers.

- A geep is a cross between a goat and a sheep. There is even a zedonk—a zebra crossed with a donkey.

fertilization   when a sperm joins an egg to form a new individual
gene   information in living things that tells how they will grow and develop

Hope for the future?

Human technology may hold a last hope for some species. The lowland gorilla of central Africa is just one animal that science may help to save. The gorillas are under threat because of poachers and the destruction of their habitat. Scientists are finding ways to raise gorilla populations. If the gorillas' eggs can be **fertilized** in test tubes, the breeding grounds of the future will be in science laboratories rather than in jungles.

Humans have caused many mammals to become extinct throughout history, and there are still many in danger around the world today. It is up to us all to save them.

Hope

The golden lion tamarin (shown below), of South America, was almost wiped out. Ninety-six percent of its forest habitat has been destroyed and thousands of tamarins have been trapped and sent to other countries as pets. It is one of the most endangered **primates,** but they have been bred in zoos, and some have been released into the wild.

◄ A project is under way to introduce captive lowland gorillas into the wild.

pollution ruining natural things with dangerous chemicals, fumes, or garbage

Find Out More

Websites

Smithsonian Institute National Zoological Park
Website with articles, information, and many photos of all kinds of animals.
nationalzoo.si.edu

Natural History Notebooks
nature.ca/notebooks

Books

Becker, John. *Bats*. Farmington, MI: Kidhaven, 2002.

Halfpenny, James C., et al. *Yellowstone Wolves in the Wild*. Helena, MT: Riverbend Publishing, 2003.

Hoyt, Erich et al. *Orca: The Whale Called Killer*. Rochester, NY: Camden House, 2003.

Solway, Andrew. *Classifying Living Things: Mammals*. Chicago: Heinemann Library, 2003.

Taylor, Barbara. *Large Mammals: Elephants, Bears and Pandas, Big Cats, Whales and Dolphins*, Cedarville, IL: Lorenz Books, 2003.

Unwin, Mike. *From Egg to Adult: The Life Cycle of Mammals*. Chicago: Heinemann Library, 2003.

World Wide Web

If you want to find out more about mammals, you can search the Internet using keywords such as these:

- "tiger **conservation**"
- pygmy + shrew
- **marsupials**

You can also find your own keywords by using headings or words from this book. Use the following search tips to help you find the most useful websites.

Answers to "Can you guess what these are?" on page 4
Largest mammal: blue whale; tallest mammal: giraffe; smallest mammal: pygmy shrew; fastest mammal: cheetah.

Search tips

There are billions of pages on the Internet, so it can be difficult to find exactly what you want to find. For example, if you just type in "water" on a search engine such as Google, you will get a list of millions of webpages. These search skills will help you find useful websites more quickly:

- Use simple keywords instead of whole sentences.
- Use two to six keywords in a search, putting the most important words first.
- Be precise—only use names of people, places, or things.
- If you want to find words that go together, put quote marks around them.
- Use the advanced section of your search engine.
- Use the "+" sign between keywords to link them.

Where to search

Search engine

A search engine looks through a small proportion of the Web and lists all sites that match the words in the search box. It can give thousands of links, but the best matches are at the top of the list on the first page. Try google.com.

Search directory

A search directory is like a library of websites that have been sorted by a person instead of a computer. You can search by keyword or subject and browse through the different sites like you look through books on a library shelf. A good example is yahooligans.com.

Numbers of incredible creatures

Creatures (y-axis): Amphibians, Mammals, Reptiles, Birds, Fish, Arachnids, Mollusks, Insects

Number of species (approximate): 0, 20,000, 40,000, 60,000, 80,000, 100,000, 120,000, 140,000, 160,000, 180,000, 1,000,000

Glossary

adapt   gradually change to survive in a particular habitat

algae   types of simple plant without stems that grow in water or wet places

altitude   height above sea level

amphibian   animal with a backbone that lives in water and on land, such as a frog

antibody   chemical in the body's cells that fights germs

bill   jaws and beak of a bird

blubber   layers of fat that protect whales and seals and keep them warm

breed   produce offspring

camouflage   color or pattern that matches the background

carbon dioxide   gas that animals breathe out

carnivore   meat-eater

carrion   dead, rotting flesh

cell   tiny building block that makes up all living things

chamber   space inside an organ or body

colony   group of animals living together

conservation   taking care of something that is in danger, such as land, to keep it from being damaged

digestive system   organs in the body that break down food to absorb nutrients

echolocation   bouncing high-pitched sounds off objects to help figure out where to go

embryo   tiny group of growing cells formed from a fertilized egg

endangered   at risk of disappearing forever

environment   natural surroundings

evolve   develop and change over time

exhausted   worn out, with all energy gone

extinct   died out, never to return

fertilization   when a sperm joins an egg to form a new individual

gene   information in living things that tells how they will grow and develop

gestation   time from when an egg is fertilized to when the baby is born

gladiator   person in ancient Rome who would fight for others' entertainment

gland   part of the body that makes hormones and other substances

gnaw   nibble at tough food

graze   eat grass and plants

habitat   natural home of an animal or plant

herbivore   animal that only eats plants

hibernate   "close down" the body and rest when it is too cold or dry

incisor   cutting tooth in the front of the mouth

infrasonic   very low-pitched sounds that humans cannot hear

insectivore   insect-eater

invertebrate   animal without a backbone

joey   baby kangaroo

krill   tiny shrimplike animals that swim in large numbers in the sea

limb   arm or leg

magnetic field   pulling force from Earth's North and South poles

mammary glands   parts for making milk in the bodies of female mammals

marrow   soft, fatty jelly inside bones

marsupial   mammal with a pouch for raising its young

mate   when a male and a female animal come together to produce young

midwife   nurse who helps a mother when she gives birth

migration   traveling long distances in search of food or to breed

monotreme   mammal that lays eggs

muscular   having strong muscles

navigation   figuring out the right way to to get somewhere

nerves   fibers that carry messages between the brain and other parts of the body

nourishment   important nutrients provided by food

nutrient   important substance found in food and needed by the body

omnivore   animal that eats both plants and animals

ovary   part of the female's body where the eggs are made

oviduct   tube inside a female down which her eggs pass

oxygen   one of the gases in air and water that all living things need

placenta   organ inside a pregnant female mammal that feeds the growing baby

poach   illegally kill and steal wild animals

pollution   ruining natural things with dangerous chemicals, fumes, or garbage

predator   animal that hunts and eats other animals

prey   animal that is killed and eaten by other animals

primate   animal with thumbs, eyes on the front of its head, and a large brain

programmed   has behavior that is "built in" or automatic

protein   nutrient in food that is used by the body for growth and repair

rabies   disease caught from bites that can cause death

regurgitate   throw up digested food

reptile   cold-blooded animal with scales, such as a snake or lizard

rodent   mammal with gnawing front teeth that keep growing

rumen   part of stomach of some herbivores

rut   when male deer fight and lock antlers to win a female as a mate

saliva   juices made in the mouth to help chewing and digestion

scavenger   animal that feeds off scraps and prey killed by others

scent   trail left by an animal that others can smell and follow

species   type of animal or plant

sperm   male sex cell

suffocate   choke or die from being unable to breathe

territory   area defended by a particular animal

ultimate   final one, with nothing to beat it

umbilical cord   cord that joins the embryo to the placenta inside the mother

unique   only one of its kind; nothing else like it

uterus   womb; where a baby grows inside its mother

venom   poison

vertebrate   animal with a backbone

warm-blooded   able to keep the body warm even if the outside temperature is cold

water-repellent   able to keep water out

weaned   coming off mother's milk

wingspan   distance from one wing tip to the other with both wings fully stretched

WWF   (World Wildlife Federation) international organization that works to protect endangered species

Index